The KNOW-NONSENSE Guide to MONEY

Written by Heidi Fiedler

Illustrated by Brendan Kearney

Brimming with creative inspiration, how-to projects, and useful information to enrich your everyday life, quarto.com is a favorite destination for those pursuing their interests and passions.

© 2017 Quarto Publishing Group USA Inc.
Illustrations © 2017 Brendan Kearney

First published in 2017 by Walter Foster Jr., an imprint of The Quarto Group.
100 Cummings Center, Suite 265D, Beverly, MA 01915, USA.
T (978) 282-9590 **F** (978) 283-2742 **www.quarto.com** • **www.walterfoster.com**

Walter Foster Jr. titles are also available at discount for retail, wholesale, promotional, and bulk purchase. For details, contact the Special Sales Manager by email at specialsales@quarto.com or by mail at The Quarto Group, Attn: Special Sales Manager, 100 Cummings Center, Suite 265D, Beverly, MA 01915, USA.

ISBN: 978-0-7603-7940-0

Written by Heidi Fiedler
Illustrated by Brendan Kearney

10 9 8 7 6 5 4 3 2 1

TABLE OF CONTENTS

INTRODUCTION

f understanding **money** seems boring, or you're looking for a funny guide to finances, you're in the right place. This book tackles the **key concepts** you need to know to earn, save, spend, and share money wisely.

Whether you're rolling in cash or counting pennies, money is important.

- It lets us exchange our precious time and energy for things like hamburgers, tutus, and skateboards, and services like getting a haircut or taking piano lessons.

- Money makes it easier to track the value of all these things.

- It also helps us know who owes what to whom.

Sound like nonsense? Fear not! By the end of this book, you'll have a wealth of new knowledge and be clear on the difference between a **debit card** and a **credit card**, understand how you can **earn** more money, and see why **sharing** and **saving** are just as important as **spending**.

WHAT IS MONEY?

Thousands of years ago, if you wanted seeds for your farm and you had an extra cow, you could simply swap with a friendly farmer. For most of history, people bartered, or traded, one thing for another. But what if you didn't have something other

people wanted? Or you needed to trade something but weren't sure how much it was worth? It didn't take people long to start using shells, beads, and grain as currency, or money. Today we use metal coins and paper money. There's even electronic money that lets people digitally exchange money without physically trading a thing. Whatever form it takes, money is what we use to pay people for their work and buy the things we need or want. Ka-ching!

COINS

A coin is a flat piece of metal that is used as money.

Around 1000 BCE, **coins** replaced the stones, shells, and cattle that were once used as money. The change first happened in China, then spread throughout the world. Today most coins are metal, but materials such as leather and porcelain have also been used. American coins include pennies, nickels, dimes, and quarters. Other countries use different currencies like pesos, pounds, euros, and yuans. (See page 18 to learn more about exchanging currencies.) Each has its own set of coins. What do all these little pieces of metal have in common? They're all useful for paying small amounts. But they're heavy to carry—although, not as heavy as cattle. "A penny for your thoughts" is definitely progress over "a cow for your thoughts!"

BILLS

A bill is a piece of paper that is used as money.

Cash is king, especially when you *are* king—although it took over 1500 years for paper money to be invented. Today **bills** come in all different amounts. Countries like The United States, The United Kingdom, Thailand, and France include portraits of important leaders on their money. Others like Spain, Zimbabwe, and Iceland show off landmarks or colorful symbols.

But the beauty of bills goes beyond the artwork. Paper money is lightweight, easier to carry than coins, and fun to throw around, especially at king-sized parties. (Warning: you might want to stick to throwing smaller bills!)

CHECKS

A check (or cheque) is a special piece of paper that directs a bank to pay money as instructed.

Unless you're a game show winner, **checks** are easy to carry. And as long as you have the money in your account, you can write them for any amount. That makes them useful, whether you're a millionaire or a zilch-ionaire. Checkbooks include a log, so you can easily track the money that comes into and out of your account. Balancing your checkbook this way lets you know how much money you have at any moment.

However, if you've ever stood behind someone writing a check at the market, you know the process is slow. Plus, it can take weeks for checks to arrive in the mail and be cashed by banks. The worst part is if you get a check, you won't know if the money is truly yours until you try to cash it. If the check writer doesn't have the money in their account, the check will *bounce*, or won't be processed. Bouncing a check may sound like a game, but it's never fun when it happens to you!

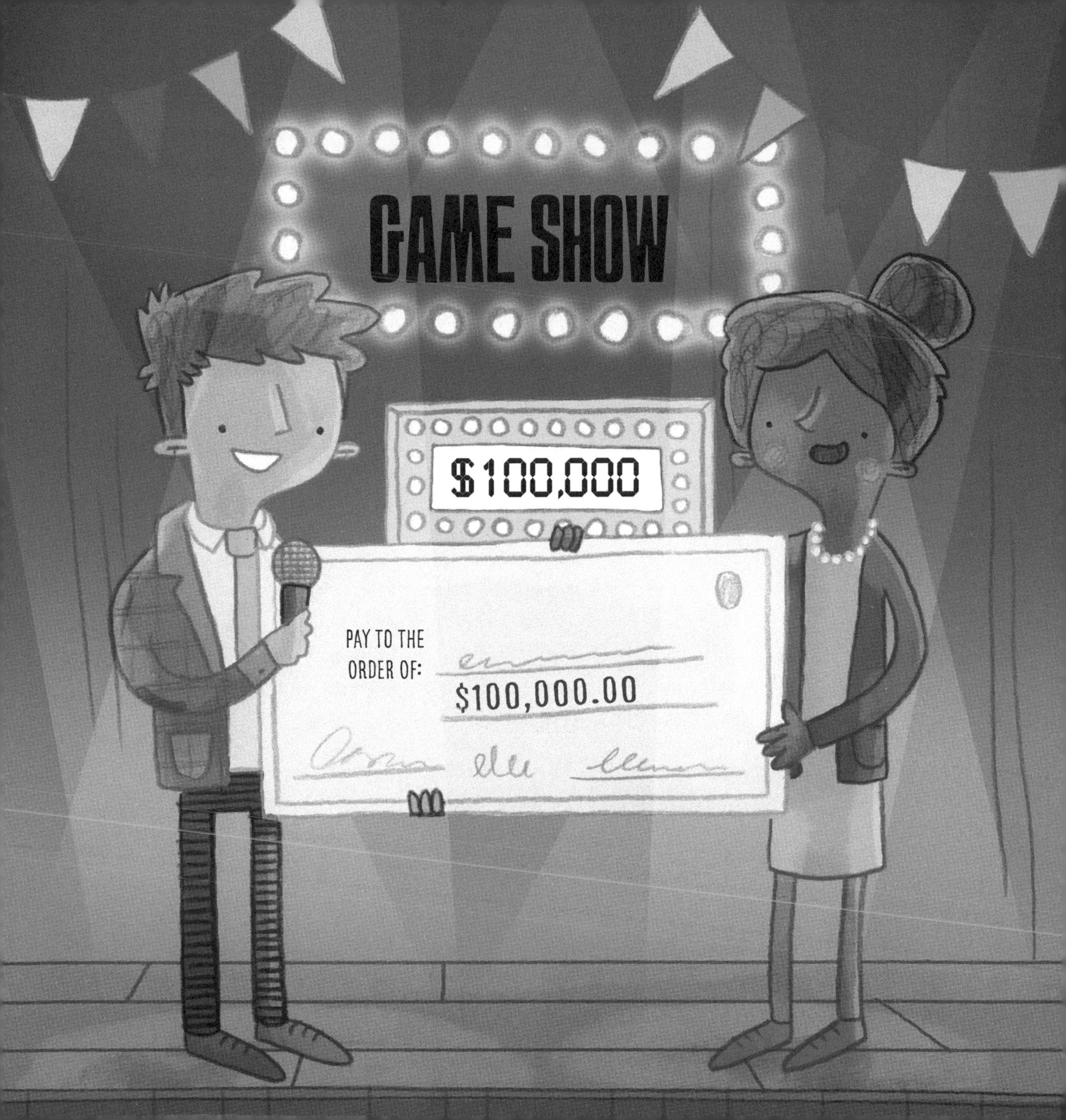
GAME SHOW
$100,000
PAY TO THE
ORDER OF:
$100,000.00

PLASTIC

Debit cards, credit cards, and gift cards are all types of plastic money.

Buying rockets, space suits, and other gear at astronomical prices can be a blast. But what if you don't have the cash? A **debit card** gives stores and companies permission to take money directly from your bank account. Or you could use a **credit card**, which lets you buy things now and pay for them later at a slightly higher cost. (See page 60 to learn more about credit.) A **gift card** is worth a certain amount of money and gives you the ability to choose your own gift and buy it from a specific store.

All these cards are easy to slip in your pocket and give you access to large sums of money. Just remember, the same thing that makes them easy to carry with you makes them just as easy to be lost or stolen—by humans or aliens!

BITCOINS

Bitcoins are a digital form of money used in online exchanges.

When you want to travel light, there's no easier way to pay than with electronic money. **Bitcoins** are a new form of digital currency. People like them because they can be used in every country and transferred directly from person to person. All you need to send money is a computer or a phone—no bank required. There's also no credit card company to take a cut of the money that's being transferred.

There is a massive network of people around the world checking to make sure no one lies about how much money they have or tries to spend the same bits of money more than once. Maybe it should be called *trustcoin*?

EXCHANGE RATE

The exchange rate is the ratio used to convert one currency to another.

When you're traveling around the world, you'll want to spend money on everything from souvenirs to eating dinner. You might even get brave and try snails! But you'll need different money to go gourmet because most countries have their own currency. It's important to know that the prices will be in the local currency, not in dollars (or the currency you usually use).

You can trade your money either at the airport or at a bank using the **exchange rate**. The exchange rate tells you how much money your dollars are worth in the local currency. So if you want to eat escargot (aka snails!) in France, and it cost 25 euros, that's really closer to 30 dollars. Remember to check the exchange rate when you arrive—the number is always changing! This week 1 dollar might equal 1 euro or .5 pounds, but next week 1 dollar might equal 2 euros or 2 pounds.

EARNING

If money makes the world go around, how do you get more of it? You might find a few quarters in the couch cushions or receive a gift card for your birthday, but the surest way to get money is to earn it. People earn money in exchange for the work they do or the services they provide. Some people earn their dough by baking bread, while others sweep floors, build new buildings, or conduct an orchestra. Read on to find out how you can get in on the action.

INCOME

Income is the money we earn from doing work, making investments, and owning things of value.

Want to grow your bank account? Add **income**! An allowance is one type of income. You can also earn money by getting a job. You might have to create your own job or convince someone to hire you, but the good news is, the more work you do, the more income you'll have.

Experts recommend finding several different ways to earn money, so if one flow of money dries up, another will still be there to support you. Farmers plant lots of different fruits and vegetables to be sure they will always have at least one source of income growing. You could sell food from your garden, tutor a friend, or rent out your bejeweled birthday tiara to neighbors. Or why not follow in farmers' footsteps and do all three?

EARNING POWER

Earning power is the ability people have to earn money based on their income, career path, lifestyle, and age.

When you envision the future, do you imagine yourself being the boss and working long hours in an office? Or would you rather have the freedom to take leisurely lunch breaks and walk home early? Maybe you hope to own a skyscraper, or perhaps you just want to earn enough money to buy a car. When you're choosing a job, it helps to know what kind of work you like to do, but it also helps to think about how much money you will need to support your dreams. Some jobs, like being a window washer, are fun to do, but they don't pay very much. Other jobs, like being a firefighter, may not pay well in the beginning, but once you have more experience, your salary goes up quickly. That gives you the power to earn more and follow your dreams—however wildly expensive they may be.

ON AVERAGE, WINDOW WASHERS MAKE $20,000 TO $50,000 PER YEAR.

ON AVERAGE, FIREFIGHTERS MAKE $50,000 TO $65,000 PER YEAR.

ENTREPRENEUR

An entrepreneur is someone who takes on the risk of running a business.

If you want to earn more money, but don't want to wait for someone to hire you, you can start your own business. Maybe you'll wash dogs, become a neighborhood bike messenger, open an art gallery in your backyard, or sell tickets to a circus with all your friends. **Entrepreneurs** are always coming up with new ways to make money. Then they do everything they can to make it happen. Sometimes it works out, and they strike gold. Other times, they spend more than they make. But it only takes one great idea done in the right way to make the risk worthwhile.

PROFIT AND LOSS

Profit is the money that remains after losses are subtracted from earnings.

Lemonade stands are so last year. Selling sweets is the new way to make some dough. But will you turn a profit or lose money trying? Entrepreneurs spend a lot of time thinking about how much it costs to make something, how much they can sell an item for, and what kind of profit will be left over. It might cost $100 to buy the right kind of oven and flour. If you charge $2.00 per doughnut, and you sell 75 doughnuts, you'll earn $150 total. That means in this business, there's $50 profit with $0 lost. Invest your profits wisely, and that's some sweet, sweet money!

A PROFIT-AND-LOSS REPORT BREAKS DOWN HOW MUCH IT COSTS TO MAKE A PRODUCT AND HOW MUCH MONEY IS EARNED SELLING IT.

PROFIT-AND-LOSS REPORT

DOUGHNUTS SOLD $2.00 X 75= $150.00

COST OF FLOUR   -$25.00

COST OF OVEN   -$75.00

PROFIT $50.00

CROWDFUNDING

Crowdfunding is the act of asking for money from a large number of people who want to help start a project.

Want to get your latest get-rich-quick idea off the ground? **Crowdfunding** is a popular way to raise money for creative projects and new businesses. Websites like Kickstarter and Indiegogo help friends, fans, and other investors donate money. The process requires entrepreneurs to know how much cash they need to fund a project, figure out how they will spend the money, and find ways to reward those who invest. Crowdfunding isn't as easy as asking pretty please, but when a campaign is successful it means you already have an audience excited about your product. And then it's up, up, and away!

BACK AN OUT-OF-THIS-WORLD PROJECT, AND YOU JUST MIGHT ZOOM AWAY WITH YOUR OWN JET PACK!

SAVING

We all have lots of things we want, need, or crave right now. The way we feel today seems very important. But what will you want, need, or crave tomorrow, next week, next year, or even in 50 years? Saving is the act of putting money aside for future use. Opening a savings account at a bank or credit union is a safe way to store and grow your money. The more you can put aside, the better. Your future self will thank you!

FINANCIAL GOALS

A financial goal is something you want to try to do with your money in the future.

Reaching a **financial goal** is like hitting a hole in one. It takes practice and attention, and it feels so good once you reach it. The best way to set financial goals is to envision what you will want and need in the future. Walk through your ideal day. Where are you living? What are you wearing? What kind of food are you eating? Who are you talking to? What type of work are you doing? What parts of your vision will you need money for? This will help you set goals that will make living your dreams a real possibility.

You might not have the money to pay for all your goals right away. Short-term goals like buying a new video game may require saving for a few weeks or months. Bigger goals like paying for college or living in Japan may take more effort. But you can't reach your goals if you don't know what they are. Start moving toward them now, and soon you'll be saying "Score!"

BANKS

A bank is a place that holds, loans, transfers, and exchanges money.

Banks are nothing to snort at. They're a safe place to save your money. And they loan money to people (not pigs). Banks also make it easy to write checks and use debit cards—they promise to pay the bills we sign. Credit unions are similar, but formed by people (not pigs) who work together or live in the same area. Because everyone has something in common, members are more likely to trust and loan each other money, with less fees than larger banks. All banks guarantee your money will be there when you want it. The money is stored in a locked vault, and you can only take your money out with a password that proves you're you. That makes it safer than any piggy bank. Oink!

INTEREST

Interest is money paid by a bank to someone who has money in a bank account.

Saving may sound boring, but it's definitely in your best interest to try it. When you put money in a savings account, your bank lends the money to other people who want to buy houses, start businesses, or go to college. In return, the bank pays you **interest**, a small amount of money based on the amount of money in your savings account. The interest rate is tied to how many people are borrowing money and how much money the bank has to lend.

Whatever the interest rate, if you don't spend any money in your savings account, you might leave the bank with more money than you started with. Makes saving money in a bank sound pretty interesting, no? (Turn to page 60 to see what interest looks like when you're borrowing instead of saving money.)

INVESTING

Investing is the process of spending money in a way that is meant to produce a profit.

Are you racing toward the future or scrambling to avoid it? **Investing** is all about spending your money in ways that will help you have more money when the future arrives. There are two main ways to invest. *Stocks* are small pieces of companies people can own and profit from. Selling stocks helps companies have the money they need to develop new products and hire people. As the company grows, its stock is worth more to its investors. Investors then use stocks to earn money for long-term goals like college, cars, and houses. A *bond* is a promise that a government or company makes to pay a specific amount of money on a certain date. Investors buy bonds knowing they will get all their money back, plus some. The practice helps governments and companies raise money to pay for large costs. Are you ready to invest in your future?

SPENDING

Once you have earned money and saved it, you're ready to spend it. Spending money lets us pay for things and experiences we need and want. But even billionaires must make choices about how to spend their money. Read on to learn how you can get the most bang for your buck!

EXPENSES

An expense is money that is spent to pay for something.

Everyone has **expenses**. Your parents might pay for expenses like food and rent. You may be responsible for other expenses like apps, school supplies, or paint for a new masterpiece. Whether you're buying a new car or just a vintage skateboard, when you're shopping around, there are choices to be made. Usually you can choose between a really extravagant version of whatever you're buying or a less expensive one. Need new wheels to get around? Teslas, Yarises, and even bicycles are all expenses. Some are just more expensive than others.

$13,700

BASIC BUT AFFORDABLE CAR

HIGH-TECH SPORTS CAR

$257,000

NEEDS VS. WANTS

A need is something you must have to survive. A want is something you would like to have but don't need.

Think about how you spend most days. What can't you live without? How much food do you eat? How much water do you drink? What clothes do you wear to stay warm? What do you do after school? How much does it cost? Knowing what you truly need and what you simply want helps sort out any nonsense in your spending, so you can avoid spending all your money on extravagant desserts or fancy electronics, and never find yourself without enough money to pay for basics like fruits and veggies, warm clothes, or pencils.

NEEDS ARE ESSENTIAL TO OUR SURVIVAL. WANTS MAKE LIFE MORE FUN TO LIVE.

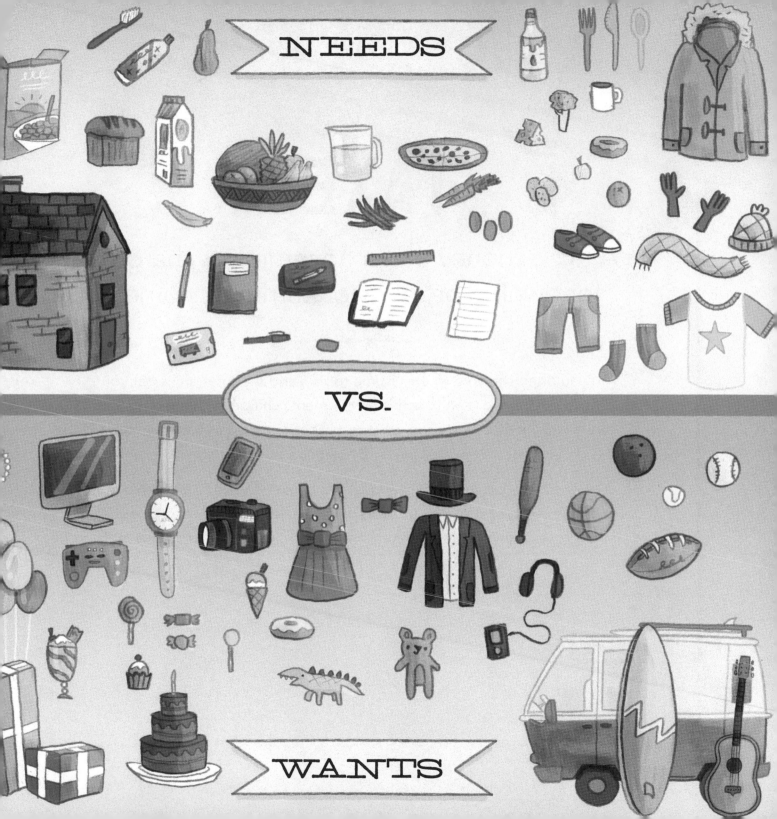

NEEDS

VS.

WANTS

TAXES

A tax is money that a government charges for owning property or earning income.

Are you often shocked when it's time to pay, and the total isn't what you expected? **Taxes** are an expense governments charge on the money we earn and the money we spend. They collect a small part of everyone's money, even companies'. Bit by bit, it adds up to a lot.

The good news is the money is meant to help everyone. Governments may use the tax we pay on a scoop of ice cream to pay for even bigger (although probably less tasty) treats like roads, schools, research, and more.

BUDGETS

A budget is a plan for using money that lists all expected income and expenses.

Just like a man and his dog, **budgets** are a smart spender's best friend. They help people know exactly how much money they have coming in and going out. A budget lists the cost of living, or the amount of money needed to pay for basics like food (for humans and pets), health care, and school, along with income and any other expenses. Making a budget each year or month helps people spend wisely, even when unexpected expenses pop up. And that deserves a bow WOW!

SPENDING LESS MONEY THAN YOU HAVE IS KNOWN AS *LIVING WITHIN YOUR MEANS.*

BUYING MEMORIES

A memory is an experience you can enjoy forever. Unlike an object, it never breaks, goes out of style, or loses value.

Replica dinosaur eggs. Underwater hammocks. Sequined scuba gear. Titanium shoelaces. There are so many things you can buy. But buy enough of those things, and you'll soon find you aren't any better off than you were before.

You can't really buy happiness, but if you want to try, the best way to spend your money is on memories, not things. It could be as simple as having a picnic with friends or as high-minded as taking a class on origami. Either way, you'll never forget the experience. Low on cash? Try eating dinner in complete darkness or hunting for rainbows after a storm. Happy spenders choose new experiences over things, which is nonsense you know you'll want to remember!

SHARING

Sharing is the act of dividing what you have and giving it others.

One for you, and one for me…everyone gets a little something. That's what makes **sharing** so popular. You can share your money, time, or energy with friends, family, or anyone who needs your help. You can donate part of your income to charities you care about. Or you can focus on making the people in your life feel special. Simple handmade gifts and thoughtful presents can let your favorite people know how much you love them.

It doesn't take much money to make a difference. And if you've ever given a gift, you know it can be even more fun than receiving one.
Now that's news that's worth sharing!

BORROWING

In the past, people bartered or traded to meet all their needs. Today people still negotiate trades, but now that there's currency, they also borrow money. They may get money from a friend or a bank by asking to pay the loan back with interest. The loan helps them pay for things they couldn't afford otherwise. The truth is borrowing makes the world go around, whether we're trading tools, ideas, or money.

DEBT

Debt is money that is owed to another person or bank.

Welcome home…to a loan? When it's time to buy something big, like a house, or pay for something expensive, like college tuition, many people borrow money from a bank. A *mortgage* is a loan that is used to buy a house. You can also get a *business loan* or a *student* loan. These **debts** help families pay for things they never could if they had to save up all the money in advance.

Some debt isn't as helpful. Owing money on a credit card or taking out a loan for something frivolous (like a fancy car) can lead to problems. But taking on debt so you can own a home that will one day sell for even more money than you bought it? SOLD!

CREDIT

Credit is the amount of money a bank or company will let someone borrow.

When you buy something on **credit**, you are borrowing money from a bank or credit card company with a promise to pay it back in the future with *interest*, a fee for using the bank or credit card company's money. Having a lot of credit can be useful in emergencies or when you need to buy something large, such as a house or a college education, that you can pay back slowly, as it adds value to your life. But it's easy to take out a loan that's too big or spend more than you can pay back, especially when you add in the interest charges. Eek! With that in mind, many people decide it's better to get their cheddar elsewhere. Others tiptoe toward credit very, very carefully.

CREDIT CAN BE A TEMPTING TRAP.

A NOTE TO KNOW-IT-ALLS

Now that you know about everything from **income** to **investing**, you can sort out the nonsense about **what makes someone wealthy**. When you know how money works, it's easy to see that money doesn't have anything to do with someone's worth. Of course money is important, but **the best things in life are free**. Laughing with friends, singing a silly song, and squishing your toes in the mud don't cost a thing. And that makes us all rich!

ALSO IN THIS SERIES

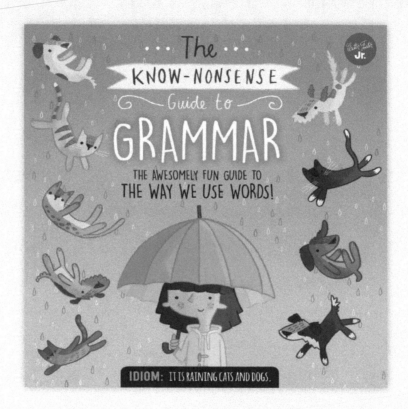

Fuzzy on punctuation? Bamboozled by adverbs? Perplexed by the difference between idioms and irony? *The Know-Nonsense Guide to Grammar* is packed with simple definitions, memorable examples, and quirky illustrations that make the rules of language easy to understand.

CPSIA information can be obtained
at www.ICGtesting.com
Printed in the USA
LVHW070929290722
724437LV00014B/14